Grandma Explains: "Who is God?"

Diane Pacheco

ISBN: 979-8-88640-869-0 (sc)
ISBN: 979-8-88640-870-6 (hc)
ISBN: 979-8-88640-871-3 (e)

One Galleria Blvd., Suite 1900, Metairie, LA 70001
1-888-421-2397

Kaylee
Taylor
Janessa
Four and a half years old.
Two years old.
Four and a half years old.

Hi girls,
come sit in
a circle please.
I would like to
talk to you
about "God".

God is our Heavenly Father!

God made all the stars and the moon and the sun and the clouds and all the oceans.

But, who knows
what the
greatest thing
God ever made
is?

Kaylee
Taylor
Janessa
The moon?

Kaylee
Taylor
Janessa
The Sun?
The Sun?

no girls, the love of His life and the love of His heart is us.

Kayla
Taylor
Janessa
God made us?
BELIEVE
BELIEVE
BELIEVE
BELIEVE

Yes Kaylee,
God made
us.

Kaylee
Taylor
Janessa
us
Grammy

Does anyone
know the names
of the first two
people God made
were?

Kaylee
Taylor
Janessa
I don't know, Grammy
BELIEVE
BELIEVE
BELIEVE
BELIEVE

Kaylee
Taylor
Janessa
Tell us,
tell us
Grammy.

Kaylee
Taylor
Janessa
Tell us Grammy.
BELIEVE
BELIEVE
BELIEVE
BELIEVE

There names
were Adam
and Eve.

Does anyone
know why
God made
us?

Kaylee
Taylor
Janessa
Why Grammy?

God made
people so He
could love us
and we could
love Him.

God wants us to be His family.

Kaylee
Taylor
Janessa
But, we already have a family.

We do have families, but if God didn't make people, we would not have our families.

Kaylee
Taylor
Janessa
Grammy,
I'm so
happy God
made us.

Kaylee
Taylor
Janessa
So, God loves us like His family.

Kaylee
Taylor
Janessa
Family.
BELIEVE
BELIEVE
BELIEVE
BELIEVE

Grand ma

Yes girls, God
loves all of us.
We are His family.
And we should love
Him too.

GrandMa)

I know it's a little hard to under-stand, but God teaches us to love. I will try to teach you so you can learn and under-stand more about God and His love.

THE WORD OF GOD
THE WILL OF GOD
Taylor
God's
family.

Grandma
Yes, Taylor, we are God's family.

GOD
Kaylee
We have families and God is our family too.

Grandma

Yes, Kaylee,

God is our

family too.

THE WILL OF GOD
THE WORD OF GOD
Kaylee
Janessa
Grammy, we love God.
We love God!
THE WORD OF GOD
THE WILL OF GOD

Grand ma'

Next time I
will explain.

"How we can learn
more about
God".